I0568489

Sprouts

For Your

Food Storage

Add Nutrition and Variety

to Your Diet

Millie Copper

Disclaimer

I am not a healthcare professional. I am a mom who believes that we are on the correct path for providing nutrient-dense, nourishing foods. You should do your own research and come to your own conclusions for your healthcare and nutrition, along with consulting a healthcare professional. I highly recommend contacting the Chapter Leader of your local Weston A. Price Foundation to ask about a list of healthcare providers.

This text contains affiliate links for Traditional Cooking School by GNOWFGLINS (www.TraditionalCookingSchool.com). If you make a purchase that originated from this document, I will receive a small commission. Your cost will be the same, and I greatly appreciate your support!

Copyright © 2022 CU Publishing LLC

ISBN-13: 978-1-957088-13-6

All Rights Reserved

Material is not to be copied, shared, or republished without prior written consent of the author. All methods/formulas are original or noted as inspired/adapted.

Table of Contents

Introduction

Sprouts are an easy, cheap, and tasty vegetable that anyone can grow. They require little space and can be done without any special equipment. Because the original product grows during the sprouting process, this is a great way to stretch a small amount into a larger amount. Sprouting is especially wonderful during winter when local produce is unavailable.

In 2008, after reading about the health benefits of soaking, souring, and sprouting, I became a sprouting fool! Sprouts are a live food and are eaten whole. When kept raw, they're loaded with enzymes, packed with nutrition, and are easily digested.

While specific nutrients vary based on the type of sprout, sprouting generally increases vitamins A, C, and B, plus they're an excellent source of vitamin K, folate, calcium, potassium, magnesium, and fiber.

During the dark days of winter, when our garden is under a blanket of snow, sprouts give us homegrown fresh greens. Combining these homegrown greens with stored vegetables and fruits (or grocery store purchases) is a fabulous treat. And with sprouts being so easy to grow, you don't even need a green thumb to have your own countertop winter "garden."

Another great benefit of sprouts is their digestibility. Do you have stomach issues when eating grains or legumes? Sprouting makes them much easier to digest by reducing phytic acid and breaking down the antinutrients. This can help not only make the grains and legumes easier on the gut but can also improve nutrition. Many people even find that sprouting their beans eliminates embarrassing side effects.

Some people who are sensitive to gluten are able to consume *sprouted* gluten-containing grains because the sprouting predigests some of the gluten. Disclaimer: you should always consult your physician regarding food sensitivities and allergies.

Sprouts are incredibly versatile. They can not only be used as condiments for salads or sandwiches but can also be added to smoothies or baked into bread, crackers, main dishes, and even desserts.

Grains, such as wheat and rice, along with beans, are very popular food storage items. Adding sprouting to your collection of preparation techniques will give you extra meal options while increasing nutrition. Sprouting small seeds, such as alfalfa and radish, provides greens in what could be a low-vegetable diet. Storing an assortment of raw nuts for sprouting can also add variety to food storage.

Storage (Pre-Sprouting)

Proper storage of the dormant seeds can give you a shelf life of several years and is essential for maximizing germination potential.

Ideally, seeds, grains, and legumes should be stored in a cool, dark, and dry location. Using quart, half-gallon, or gallon-sized mason jars works well for protecting your seeds from critters.

For long-term storage, using mylar bags with oxygen absorbers, stored in lidded buckets, can give many years of viable grains and legumes for future sprouts.

Smaller seeds, such as radish and broccoli, and grains like quinoa (a pseudo grain) store well via a vacuum seal system. Refer to the source where you purchase your seeds for individual shelf lives.

When properly stored, many varieties are viable for several years. You can even consider saving seeds to use not only for planting in the garden but also for sprouts.

Note: Nightshades (tomatoes, peppers, eggplants, potatoes, and more) contain alkaloids, which are mildly toxic. While most people can safely eat these fruits and vegetables in normal amounts, there is concern with sprouting. Because of this, I choose to err on the side of caution and not sprout nightshades.

Be aware that older seeds, grains, and legumes may not sprout as well as newer varieties. I've compared ten-year-old quinoa from my food storage to newly purchased quinoa. While the food storage quinoa did soften and form slight tales, the new quinoa was quicker to sprout and had longer tails. The food storage quinoa still tastes fine and works well for most recipes. Likewise, older lentils do not sprout as quickly or develop as long of tails as fresher lentils.

According to the Utah State University Extension website, there have not been any scientific studies on vitamin loss from long-term storage of beans. However, they do predict that, after five years, there may not be any vitamins present.

The Extension does not specify if storage in mylar bags with oxygen absorbers will help with vitamin conservation. It does specify that hot, humid temperatures will cause faster vitamin loss. While you may lose vitamins with long-term storage, protein, minerals, and carbohydrates should be unaffected.

Because of the natural oils in nuts, they do not lend themselves to long-term storage. Nuts stored in their shell do have a longer shelf-life than shelled nuts.

We've successfully stored whole almonds in vacuum-sealed bags for over a year. They need to be kept cool and in a dark location. The freezer is also a good long-term option for nuts. We have a bag of walnuts from my husband's grandma's tree that have been in the freezer for a couple of years. The flavor is the same now as the day we first froze them.

Basic Sprouting Guidelines

- Start with clean equipment. Wash your sprouting device between uses. Sterilize as needed.
- See the recommendations in the "Safety" chapter regarding treating your seeds.
- Soak first (usually).
- Drain off the soaking water. This can be saved to water houseplants, bushes, gardens, etc.
- Choose the correct sprouting device for the size of the seeds. Need to conserve water? Check the "Sprouts While Traveling" chapter for options on sprouters that use less water.
- Every 8 to 12 hours, rinse, rinse, rinse, and rinse some more in cool water. During hot and humid weather, rinse every 6 to 8 hours (schedule permitting) and ensure you are using cool water.
- After rinsing, drain well. Tap gently or vigorously, depending on your sprouting device, to remove as much water as possible. Set the device in a manner that encourages continued draining.
- Air is important! Don't lock your sprouts away during the sprouting process. They need to breathe.
- Know how to best store the finished sprouts. In general, most well-rinsed and well-drained sprouts will keep in the fridge for several days. Some sprouts, such as wheat and quinoa, do not store as well as sprouted vegetables do. Make small batches to consume within a day or two, or dehydrate to use as sprouted flour.

Sprouting Devices

There are many, many basic and specialty sprouting containers. For years, I've used a simple mason jar with a metal screen when sprouting small seeds, securing the screen with the band that came with the jar. For larger grains and legumes, I often sprout in a half-gallon jar or a colander. When traveling, I use a hemp bag or have even been known to create a sprouting container out of a plastic water bottle or gallon jug.

I recommend starting with a simple, inexpensive sprouting set up. As you make sprouting a regular part of your routine, you may wish to explore other sprouting devices. You're sure to find a sprouter that works well for you and best fits into your lifestyle.

Essentially, your sprouting device can be simple or fancy. Whichever container you choose, be sure to clean it well and sterilize between uses.

Find a complete list of sprouting devices on the resources page: HomespunOasis.com/Sprouting.

Safety

Commercial sprouts have been linked to outbreaks of salmonella and E. coli. Alfalfa, radish, and mung bean have frequently been found as the source of these outbreaks, but all raw sprouts pose a risk.

Clean practices, which include washing your hands before coming into contact with your sprouts or sprouting equipment, and also keeping your sprouting equipment clean and sterilized will help prevent any issues.

Many people run their dishwasher-safe sprouting devices through the dishwasher to sterilize.

Plain, unscented bleach is another common sterilization method. Use 3 tablespoons per quart of water, let soak for 10 to 20 minutes, then rinse well.

I use white distilled vinegar. Add 2 cups of water with ½ cup white distilled vinegar to your sprouter, let soak for half an hour, then rinse in clear water. Like bleach, vinegar is known to kill both salmonella and E. coli.

Some people choose to use only boiling water to kill contaminants. Bring the water to a rolling boil, add your sprouting device(s), and let boil 1 minute. Turn off and let cool.

While keeping your sprouting device clean and sanitized is an important process of sprouting, most foodborne illness outbreaks have been linked back to the seeds

Purchasing certified pathogen-free seeds is the first step to having a safe finished product.

- The University of California Publication 8151 recommends Sprout People and Burpee Seed Co. as two sources of safe seeds.
- K-State Research and Extension along with the University of Missouri Extension (in their publication Sprouting Seeds at Home - Safely Extension Food Safety Fact Sheet - July 2018) list International Sprout Supplier and Caudill Seeds as suppliers who have attended their Sprout Safety Alliance training for pathogen-free seeds.

In addition to purchasing pathogen-free seeds, both publications recommend treating the seed.

This treatment is accomplished by heating the seeds on the stovetop in a solution of 3% hydrogen peroxide preheated to 140°F. The temperature should be maintained for 5 minutes.

When doing this in small batches, use a small mesh strainer to hold the seeds in the water (swirl the strainer at one-minute intervals to ensure each seed is treated) or tie the seeds in a small cheesecloth sachet, moving it around to ensure each seed is reached with the peroxide solution. Rinse the seeds with clear, running water after the five-minute peroxide bath, then proceed with soaking.

Please note: this information for treating seeds in peroxide appears to be limited to green sprouts, such as radish, mung bean, broccoli, etc., which are commonly eaten raw. This does not seem to apply to grains (wheat, rice, quinoa) or hard beans like pinto, chickpea, or black beans. Lentils are also not listed in any advisories from my research. Should you choose to eat any variety of sprouts raw, you may wish to consider treating those sprouts with the peroxide solution as recommended.

Even with these precautions listed above, there is still a recommendation that young children, elderly persons, or persons with weakened immune systems should not eat raw sprouts.

I believe sprouting enthusiasts should be aware of these guidelines. From this position of knowledge, you are free to make your own choices. I am not advocating unsafe practices. Each person must understand the risks and make their own choices.

Tips and Troubleshooting

Most sprouting issues revolve around not spending enough time tending to your sprouts. When you rinse them, you must take a few minutes to remove as much water as possible. Tap, bounce, shake, and move your sprouter to encourage draining. This will help as many seeds as possible sprout while preventing spoilage. Standing water is not your sprouts' friend.

Smelly sprouts? While a few sprouts, like broccoli, can have a stronger odor than other varieties, all should still smell pleasant. If your sprouts do not smell as they should, it's likely a drainage issue. Tap, bounce, shake, and move your sprouter each time you rinse.

Mold? Using a good-quality seed, such as those from Sprout People or Burpee Seed Co., helps eliminate mold. And are you really seeing mold, or is it cilia hairs? Cilia hairs are the root hairs common on green sprouts (radish, broccoli) and grain sprouts.

These feather-like hairs usually appear around the second or third day. The appearance of cilia is a sign your sprouts are not receiving enough water. Proper and regular rinsing (at least two or more times a day) will help with cilia hairs. After rinsing, the hairs will be less noticeable. Cilia hairs are not mold, and your sprouts are still fine.

If your sprouts smell, are slimy, and have a cobweb-like appearance spreading across many areas (not just the roots), then you probably do have mold. Molded sprouts need to be discarded.

To prevent mold on future batches, clean and sterilize your sprouter and sprouting equipment (chopsticks, towels, etc). Ensure you are using a sprouting device with proper drainage. You do not want your sprouts to sit in water. Be sure to rinse well with cool water. Tap, bounce, shake, and move your sprouter to encourage draining.

Do not place your sprouts in a closed-in area, such as a cabinet. Keep them on a countertop that's open to the air. To help avoid cross-contamination, keep sprouts away from other things you may be growing or fermenting, such as kombucha, sourdough, cheeses, kefir, and lacto-fermentation projects.

Chia and flax are mucilaginous seeds. When submerged in water, they turn into a gel. They can be sprouted using a dry method and terra cotta—think Chia Pets. A quick Google search will give you more info on working with these types of seeds.

Small Seeds

Seeds such as alfalfa, radish, broccoli, clover, and more turn a simple seed into an almost decadent vegetable.

When sprouting these small seeds, you begin with only a couple of tablespoons but end up with 5 to 10 times the amount in finished sprouts (depending on variety).

You need to use a sprouting device suited for small seeds. A jar with a mesh strainer (metal or plastic) or even a section of loosely woven cloth or pantyhose work well, as do specially designed sprouting devices.

Basic Directions for Small Seeds

1. Sort and rinse your seeds.
2. See the recommendations in the "Safety" chapter regarding treating your seeds.
3. Soak in cool water for 6 to 12 hours
4. Drain off water.
5. Rinse thoroughly.
6. Move to your chosen sprouter or add a sprouting lid. Set on an out-of-the-way countertop. Some natural light is great, but they should not be in direct sunlight.
7. Rinse and tap to smooth. Drain off water. Important! You do not want your sprouts sitting in water. Draining well keeps them from souring.
8. Rinse and drain with cool water every 8 to 12 hours (6 to 8 hours in hot, humid weather).
9. As the seeds begin to sprout, you may notice they are clumping together. Use a fork or chopstick to divide these clumps as needed. Do this at each rinsing and draining.
10. On day four, if needed, move to a location with more sunlight to help the sprouts green. Do not put in direct sunlight; this can be too hot and cook your sprouts.

11. Continue to rinse and drain every 8 to 12 hours.
12. By day five, you can begin to dehull the sprouts when you rinse by gently brushing them. Dehulling not only provides a more pleasing finished product but also helps improve storage.
13. By day six, most of your sprouts should have open green leaves. Before your final rinse, you'll want to continue dehulling, especially if you plan to store the sprouts in the fridge for more than a couple of days. Use a large bowl or a salad spinner to remove the majority of hulls. A salad spinner will eliminate step 14; spinning will dry the sprouts enough you'll be able to refrigerate them immediately.
14. Let your rinsed and dehulled (maybe) sprouts drain for 8 to 12 hours before transferring to the fridge.
15. Store in a sealed container or a plastic bag.

Dehull

Using a bowl:

Transfer your sprouts to a big bowl (use a bigger bowl than you think you'll need). Fill with cool water. Reach in and loosen the sprouts, separating them with your fingers. As you pull the clumps apart, the hulls will rise to the top. Keep working your sprouts, pushing them toward the bottom of the bowl to allow the lighter hulls to rise to the top.

Skim the hulls off the top and repeat two or three times. Return the sprouts to your sprouter or move to a colander. Give a final rinse and then drain for 8 to 12 hours before moving to the refrigerator.

Using a salad spinner:

Put the strainer container inside the solid bowl. Place in the sink. Transfer your sprouts to the strainer. Depending on the quantity of sprouts and the size of your salad spinner, you may need to divide the batch in half.

Fill with cool water. Reach in and loosen the sprouts, separating with your fingers. As you pull the clumps apart, the hulls will rise to the top. Push the sprouts down and let the hulls float out over the top. Keep working the sprouts until you have most of the hulls removed.

Lift out the strainer and compost any hulls in the solid bowl. Rinse the bowl out, then return the strainer to the solid bowl. Put the lid on the salad spinner and use according to manufacturer's directions for spinning salad. Take apart and pour the water out of the solid bowl. Repeat the spinning process two times to ensure sprouts are as dry as possible.

Small Seed Tips

Be sure to read the "Tips and Troubleshooting" chapter for common issues.

Making sure to thoroughly rinse these seeds in cool water will give you the best sprouts possible. Using a chopstick or something similar to break up the sprouts (when growing in a mason jar) is also very helpful to ensure each root is rinsed. Do not let your sprouts sit in water. They need to drain.

If you aren't happy with the results from one sprouting device, try a different option. There are so many available. For these small seeds, I've had excellent results with a mason jar with a stainless-steel, two-piece lid and with a one-piece plastic lid.

I also really like vertical sprouters. When using a vertical sprouter, the seedlings root themselves into the screen of the growing tray, eliminating the need for breaking up the sprouts.

Just like trying different sprouters for different results, try different seeds. Broccoli seeds give me much different results than alfalfa or radish. So much so, I've chosen to no longer bother with broccoli; it's not worth the frustration of having what I consider to be a lesser-quality sprout.

Grains

Grains such as wheat, rye, brown rice, millet, kamut, and more make wonderful and versatile sprouts. Quinoa, which is a seed, is often considered a grain. I'll give special instructions below for this tasty treat.

When sprouting grains, start with a larger amount than the small seeds. The yield is approximately 1.5:1. I like to start with a cup of grains and end up with approximately 1.5 cups of sprouted product.

Note: Sprouted grains continue to grow in the refrigerator, making them less than desirable for storing past a day or two. Plan to sprout only as much as you will use. Even better, sprout and dehydrate, then mill for your own sprouted flour.

Basic Directions for Grains

1. Sort and rinse your grain.
2. See the recommendations in the "Safety" chapter regarding treating your seeds.
3. Soak in cool water for 6 to 12 hours.
4. Drain off water.
5. Rinse thoroughly.
6. Move to your chosen sprouter or add a sprouting lid. Drain off water. Important! You do not want your sprouts sitting in water. Draining well keeps them from souring. I like to sprout large grains, such as wheat berries, in either a half-gallon jar (with screen or cloth on top) or in a colander with a plate underneath (to catch water) and a plate on top (to keep out dust, etc.). Millet, a small grain, works best when using a quart jar and sprouting screen or a mesh colander perched on a bowl. Set on an out-of-the-way countertop. Some natural light is great, but they should not be in direct sunlight.

7. Rinse and drain well with cool water every 8 to 12 hours (6 to 8 hours in hot, humid weather). *Note:* Grain sprouts do not need to be moved to sunlight. We do not "green" them.

8. Grains are ready to harvest on day two or three, when they have short roots. *Note:* Some grains show very little root. Brown rice tends to bulge at the germ but don't always develop tails. Hulled millet softens and swells but, again, shows little tail.

9. Drain sprouts well. They should be nearly dry before moving to the refrigerator.

10. Use well-drained sprouted grains within 48 hours or expect to see longer roots and maybe grass shoots.

11. I've successfully frozen sprouted wheat and sprouted brown rice to use at a later time in cooked recipes.

Dehydrating Sprouted Grains in a Dehydrator

1. Transfer thoroughly rinsed and drained sprouts to dehydrator trays covered with parchment paper or a liner specific to your brand of dehydrator.

2. Spread as much grain as possible in a single layer.

3. Dry for 2 hours, then gently move the grains around, returning to a single layer.

4. Continue to dehydrate until dry. Depending on my day, I may check and move them around every few hours. The process may take 8 to 24 hours. Test for dryness by tasting. The grain should be hard and crunchy.

5. Turn off the dehydrator and allow the sprouted grains to cool completely before transferring to a storage container.

Dehydrating Sprouted Grains in the Oven

1. Transfer thoroughly drained sprouts to baking tray(s) in a single layer. Dry at the lowest oven temperature possible. I crack open the door of my oven to lower the temp even further. Check frequently for burning or unevenly drying grains. Stir gently each time and return to a single layer.

2. This process can take anywhere from 2 hours (if your oven temp is too high) to 10 hours. Test for dryness by tasting. The grain should be hard and crunchy.
3. Remove from oven and allow the sprouted grains to cool completely before transferring to a storage container.

Storing Sprouted, Dehydrated Grains

Keep sprouted, dehydrated grains in the freezer or transfer them to storage containers such as mylar bags with oxygen absorbers inside 5-gallon food-grade buckets with gamma seal lids. Or use other airtight containers such as glass jars. When properly stored in cool, dry, dark, and critter-free spaces, they can last many years.

Milling Sprouted Grains

Mill grains as normal by following your grain mill's instructions. Milled whole grain does not store well. It can be kept at room temperature for about a week or in the freezer for six months.

Whole Grain Berries

Wheat (all varieties), spelt, einkorn, oat groats, and unhulled barley are all sprout friendly. There is no deviation from the basic instructions for grains.

Oat groats do need special attention when purchasing. You want to ensure you buy oats specifically designed for sprouting. Rolled oats and other processed oats are often steam or heat treated and will not sprout.

Whole grain berries are often turned into grass to use in smoothies. These grasses begin their life as a kernel that is soaked and then planted (in a medium such as hemp felt) until it is 4" to 12" tall. Grasses can be grown as fodder for chicken, goats, cattle, and more.

Brown Rice

Long or short brown rice can be sprouted. Choose a mason jar with a screen or a mesh colander as your sprouting device. You want to make sure the holes are not too large so that the rice doesn't escape.

Some varieties and brands sprout better than others. Fresher rice also sprouts more readily. I look for the germ to bulge and taste at each rinsing. The rice should be soft and slightly sweet, while not overly chewy. There may or may not be noticeable tails.

All rice should be well rinsed prior to soaking and follow the basic directions for grains. White rice has the germ removed and will not sprout. Wild rice, a grass, doesn't sprout but it does open and "bloom." The split wild rice is very soft and can be eaten raw.

Millet

Hulled millet, which is widely available, has a very low success rate for sprouting. You can purchase unhulled millet from specialty sources. Or you can understand that while hulled millet won't give you beautiful sprouts, digestion and vitamins can be improved by treating it as a tailless sprout.

Choose a mason jar with a screen or a fine mesh colander as your sprouting device. You want to make sure the holes are not too large so that the millet doesn't escape. Watch for the millet to swell and taste at each rinsing.

While I rarely see sprouts, the millet does change after soaking and at each rinsing. I let it go for 2 or 3 days until it's a satisfying crispness and suitable for eating raw in salads or muesli. It's delicious.

Millet sprays, often purchased for household birds, can also be sprouted. The entire spray is soaked, rinsed well, then set in a colander to drain. Continue the process, rinsing and draining two or three times a day, until the sprouts form. Keep sprouting until it resembles grass. It's a great treat for your feathered friends!

Quinoa

Quinoa, pronounced KEEN-wah, is a gluten-free, whole-protein pseudo grain. While often referred to as a rice substitute, quinoa is a seed. For sprouting purposes, we treat it more like a grain than a small seed.

Quinoa contains saponins, a bitter, soapy tasting substance that protects the quinoa plant from fungal and insect attacks. Some people find it unpalatable or may be sensitive to it. The sprouting process helps reduce the saponins. (Saponin is also found in legumes, some vegetables, teas, amaranth seeds, and more.)

When sprouting quinoa, the yield is approximately 1.5:1. If you start with 1 cup unsprouted, you should end with approximately 1.5 cups of sprouted quinoa.

1. Rinse the quinoa well. The water may look "soapy" from the saponins. Keep rinsing until the water runs clear.
2. See the recommendations in the "Safety" chapter regarding treating your seeds.
3. Soaking is optional. Sometimes, especially if I'm on the road, I'll just give the quinoa a good rinse and begin the sprouting process. Other times, I'll soak for up to an hour. If soaking, put in a bowl or jar and cover with fresh water about an inch above the quinoa.
4. Drain well.
5. Move to your chosen sprouter or add a sprouting lid. Quinoa is a small grain, so choose an appropriate sprouter. I like to use either a mason jar with a sprouting lid or a mesh strainer perched

on a bowl. Drain off water. Important! You do not want your sprouts sitting in water. Draining well keeps them from souring.

6. Set on an out-of-the-way countertop. Some natural light is great, but they should not be in direct sunlight.

7. Continue to rinse and drain every 8 to 12 hours for two, three, or maybe four cycles. Quinoa will have tiny, sprouted roots and will still be slightly crunchy. If you sprout longer, it loses its crunch. Taste at each rinsing to find out how you like your sprouted quinoa.

8. Lightly sprouted quinoa stores well in the refrigerator. Be sure it is dry before moving to your storage container.

Grain Tips

Be sure to visit the "Tips and Troubleshooting" chapter for common issues.

Make sure to thoroughly rinse your grain in cool water to give you the best sprouts possible. I like to rinse with my sink sprayer, cover with water, and then turn off the water and give my sprouting device a shake to ensure each grain is coated before spraying again.

If you aren't happy with the results from one sprouting device, try a different option. There are so many available.

For large grains, I prefer a footed colander. Set it on a plate to catch any additional drainage and cover with a tea towel.

For smaller grains, such as rice, millet, and quinoa, I like a fine mesh strainer with a handle. The handle makes it easy to jostle the grain around. With these small grains, I spend a few extra seconds to make sure the water is removed as much as possible. I then perch the strainer above a bowl and cover with a tea towel.

Beans and Legumes

A legume is a plant that bears its seed inside a pod. The umbrella term *legumes* includes pulses (the seed is being used as a dried grain) and peanuts. Pulses are often referred to as beans. While this basic information on sprouting legumes works for most dried beans, peanuts are addressed under nuts.

Mung beans are probably the most popular legume sprout. They're also incredibly easy to sprout. But so are lentils, chickpeas, pinto beans, etc. Mung beans and lentils are a softer bean. They tend to grow a longer tail and produce a higher yield than hard beans.

Basic Directions for Legumes (Not Peanuts)

1. Sort and rinse your beans, lentils, peas, etc. Remove any debris during the sorting process and rinse until the water runs clear.
2. See the recommendations in the "Safety" chapter regarding treating your seeds.

3. Soak in cool water for 8 to 12 hours. For hard beans, such as chickpeas, pinto beans, white beans, black beans, or kidney beans, you may wish to soak for 24 hours, draining the water at the 12-hour mark and replacing with fresh. I've found this makes the beans even more digestive-tract friendly.
4. Drain off water.
5. Rinse thoroughly until the water runs clear.
6. Move to your chosen sprouter or add a sprouting lid. Rinse again. Drain off water. Important! You do not want your sprouts sitting in water. Draining well keeps them from souring.
7. Set on an out-of-the-way countertop. Some natural light is great, but they should not be in direct sunlight.
8. Continue to rinse and drain every 8 to 12 hours (6 to 8 hours if hot and humid).
9. Around day two or three, you'll start to see the tails. Chickpeas, pinto beans, black beans, kidney beans, peas, lentils, etc. are ready when the tail is 1/16" to 1/2" long. You can stop mung beans here also or continue the rinse and drain process a few more days until you have 1" tails.
10. Store the well-rinsed and well-drained legumes in the refrigerator until ready to use. They will keep for several days. For longer storage, you can rinse and drain them before returning to the fridge. As always, the sprouts should be well drained (nearly dry) before storing.
11. You can freeze sprouted hard beans (pinto, chickpea, black, etc.) to use in cooked dishes.
12. Mung bean and lentil sprouts can be enjoyed raw or lightly steamed. Chickpea, pinto beans, black beans, etc. are wonderful to use as part of a cooked main dish, such as chili.
13. Sprouted beans can be dehydrated and milled into flour. Refer to the information under grains. The instructions are the same, but beans may take longer to dehydrate.

Mung Beans

Many people have been introduced to sprouts via mung beans. While I love having them in Asian dishes at restaurants, they do not compare to mung beans sprouted at home.

The deep green color of mung beans lightens as it soaks. This lightening indicates the bean is absorbing the water—a good thing! Mung beans should soak for 12 hours (not the short end of 8 recommended under Basic Directions). These beans do not readily benefit from the extended 24-hour soak. Soak them for 12 (give or take), drain the water, give them a good rinse, then get on with the sprouting.

Mung beans can be enjoyed in stir-fries and similar dishes or eaten raw.

They can be sprouted to any length you desire. Taste at each rinsing. If you are looking for 1" long, thick tails, this could take several days. My favorite sprouting device for mung beans is a footed colander with a plate underneath (to catch excess water) and draped with a tea towel.

Lentils

These are my all-time favorite sprouts. They are so easy and make fabulous dishes. I often soak a giant batch, drain, and start the sprouting process, then start "stealing" from the batch. Those barely sprouted lentils make fabulous soups. I share more about this method in my book *Stretchy Beans: Nutritious and Economical Meals the Easy Way.*

When I'm going for a full lentil sprout, I look for tails ¼" to ½" long. I also taste at each rinsing. Sometimes the taste is what I want when the tail isn't. My favorite sprouting device for lentils is a footed colander with a plate underneath and draped with a tea towel.

Lentils can be eaten raw, lightly steamed, sauteed, or baked.

Sprouted lentils aren't just for home! We sprout on road trips, camping trips, backpacking trips, work trips, and more. Be sure to check the "Sprouts while Traveling" chapter for more information.

Hard Beans

Chickpeas, pinto beans, white beans, black beans, and kidney beans all sprout beautifully. I usually use a 24-hour soak on these, draining off the water at the halfway point and refilling with fresh. Hard beans don't sprout as readily as lentils. I taste the beans at each rinsing—except kidney beans. Read the information below on why kidney beans should NOT be eaten raw (not even one). I look for tails that are 1/16" to 1/4" long.

Sprouted pinto, chickpea (garbanzo), white, or black beans make a wonderful raw bean dip (the recipe for Simple Bean Dip is included in this book). Hard-sprouted beans take 30 minutes to an hour on the stovetop to be soft and creamy.

I recommend tasting the sprouted beans every few minutes the first time you cook a new variety. Once you get the hang of cooking with sprouted beans, try your favorite alternative-cooking methods such as the crockpot, Instant Pot (they are ready in only a few minutes), woodstove, hay box, or Sun Oven (my summertime favorite).

A special and important note about kidney beans: Raw kidney beans contain very high amounts of phytohemagglutinin, which can lead to food poisoning, including symptoms such as nausea, vomiting, and diarrhea. I rarely sprout kidney beans. When I do, I do not taste during the sprouting process; I judge the readiness by sight only. When I determine they've sprouted long enough, I bring them to a rolling boil, which I maintain for 10 minutes. Then I drain off the cooking water before adding them to a different dish or further cooking (in fresh water) on the stovetop, in the crockpot, Instant Pot, etc.

Bean and Legume Tips

Be sure to visit the "Tips and Troubleshooting" chapter for common issues.

Make sure to thoroughly rinse your beans in cool water to give you the best sprouts possible. I like to rinse with my sink sprayer, cover with water, and then turn off the water and give my sprouting device a shake to ensure each bean is coated before spraying again.

Do not let your sprouts sit in water. They need to drain.

If you aren't happy with the results from one sprouting device, try a different option. There are so many available.

For hard beans and lentils, I prefer a footed colander. Set it on a plate to catch any additional drainage and cover with a tea towel.

Don't expect every bean to sprout. Depending on the bean's age, brand, and more, some may show very long tails, some short little tails, and some simply bulge.

Nuts and Large Seeds

Nuts such as almonds, Brazil nuts, and hazelnuts, along with peanuts, may be sprouted—sort of. While often referred to as sprouts, they are really more of a soak since the process is stopped before the tails are formed.

Starting with a raw nut or peanut, giving it a soak, rinsing for a day or two, and then dehydrating results in wonderful and delicious crispy nuts. Or you can skip the dehydrating and eat the soaked nuts raw. Large seeds, such as sunflower and pumpkin, are also great as soaks.

The challenge many have when sprouting nuts is finding raw nuts or peanuts. Cashews are never sold raw and do not lend themselves to sprouting (though some people do still give cashews a short soak, no longer than 6 hours, and then roast them on the stovetop or in the oven to improve digestibility).

Almonds can be unreliable since all almonds sold as raw in the US must be pasteurized. There are two common almond pasteurization methods: "washing" the almonds with steam and fumigation of the almonds with Propylene Oxide gas (PPO). Steam-pasteurized almonds will *usually* still sprout and are the better choice for this purpose.

Nuts do swell somewhat during the sprouting/soaking process. Depending on the nut, your yield may be 1.25:1 or up to 2:1. So you could start with 1 cup of nuts and end up with 1 ¼ cup or even 2 cups. I'll be honest, while I've read about yields of 2:1, I've never achieved it. A yield of 1.5:1 is more realistic.

1. Rinse your nuts.
2. See the recommendations in the "Safety" chapter regarding treating your seeds.

3. Soak in cool water for 4 to 12 hours (see suggestions below). If desired, you can add up to 1 teaspoon of sea salt per 1 cup of nuts/seeds to the soaking water. This will add a lightly salted flavor to the final product.
4. Drain off water. Important! You do not want your sprouts sitting in water. Draining well keeps them from souring.
5. Move to your chosen sprouter or add a sprouting lid. A colander works well for nuts. Rinse and drain well.
6. Set on an out-of-the-way countertop. Some natural light is great, but they should not be in direct sunlight.
7. Continue to rinse and drain every 8 to 12 hours for two or three cycles. You are not looking for tails but may see a bulge on one end. Taste at each rinsing. You want your nuts to still be crunchy.
8. Drain as thoroughly as possible at the final rinsing.
9. Sprouted/soaked nuts can be eaten fresh, stored for several days in the refrigerator, or dehydrated for longer storage.

Soaking Times

- Sunflower seeds: 4 hours
- Pumpkin seeds: 1 to 4 hours
- Cashews: 2 to 6 hours
- Peanuts, almonds, Brazil nuts, hazelnuts: 4 to 12 hours

Dehydrating Nuts and Large Seeds

1. Transfer thoroughly rinsed and drained sprouts to dehydrator trays covered with parchment paper or a liner specific to your brand of dehydrator.
2. Spread in a single layer.
3. Dry for 2 hours, then gently move the nuts around, returning to a single layer.
4. Continue to dehydrate until dry. Depending on my day, I may check and move them around every few hours. The process may take 8 to 24 hours, depending on the nut or seed. Test for dryness by tasting. The nut or seed should be crisp and crunchy.

5. Turn off the dehydrator and allow the nuts/seeds to cool completely before transferring to a storage container.
6. Dehydrated nuts/seeds will store for several weeks at room temperature. For longer storage, move to the freezer. Nuts and large seeds are high in oils and may go rancid over time.
7. Dehydrated nuts and seeds can be processed until smooth for your own homemade nut or seed butter.

Roasting Nuts and Seeds

Roasting is a quicker option than dehydrating. It's also the recommended option for cashews. The dehydrating process is too slow and may result in a soft, slimy end product.

1. Preheat the oven to 325° Fahrenheit. Arrange the nuts/seeds in a single layer on a baking tray.
2. Bake in the oven, checking and rotating the nuts/seeds on the tray every 5 minutes. Test at each checking to prevent burning. They can quickly go from not ready to being too done.
3. Allow to cool completely before transferring to a storage container.
4. Roasted nuts/seeds will store for several weeks at room temperature. For longer storage, move to the freezer. Nuts and large seeds are high in oils and may go rancid over time.
5. Roasted nuts and seeds can be processed until smooth for your own homemade nut or seed butter.

Sprouts While Traveling

Sprouts aren't just for home. We sprout on road trips, camping trips, backpacking trips, work trips, and more.

While you could easily sprout just about anything while traveling, we tend to stick with our family favorites: radish, quinoa, and lentils. Radish sprouts are reserved for times we'll be away for longer than a week, but quinoa and lentils are perfect sprouts after only a couple of days. These sprouts also give us no-cook meal options for hotels, campgrounds, etc.

My favorite sprouting device for radish, quinoa, and other small seed sprouts while on the road is the Easy Sprout Sprouter. The way the sprouter stacks and takes up little room makes it perfect for traveling.

The sprouter doubles as a soaker. Insert the growing vessel (the piece with the holes in it) into the solid base (use the small seed insert for small seeds, quinoa, or millet) then fill with water. When the soaking time is up, lift out the growing vessel and discard the water.

So easy!

Then proceed with your rinsing step by running water over the seeds in the growing vessel.

If you are camping or have limited water, you could put the growing vessel back in the solid base and refill with water (make sure there is about double the water as seeds/sprouts), then swirl the growing vessel around the solid base to wet all the seeds/sprouts. This is easiest when the seeds are young. As the growing vessel fills, you may need to use a utensil to help move the sprouts in the water.

Drain off all the water, tap and move your growing vessel to help remove as much water as possible, then place back in the solid base until the next rinse cycle.

If growing greens, you'll still want to give them some sunlight (see Basic Directions for Small Seeds). The sprouter will allow enough light through.

The Easy Sprout includes a lid to store your finished sprouts in the solid base and tuck them in the fridge.

You could use the Easy Sprout for sprouting lentils, but you won't have a very large yield. I prefer using a hemp bag for them. The bag folds flat for traveling. For draining, it can hang from the hotel sink or shower or even a backpack. The hemp bag provides great drainage and air circulation.

To use a hemp bag to sprout lentils, add your sorted lentils to the bag and tie the top. Rinse under clear running water or dip in a bowl of water to remove any residue on the legumes. Fill a bowl, basin, bucket—anything that will hold water—with clean water. Place your tied hemp bag in the water. Tuck the bag over so water doesn't wick up the bag and out onto the counter. Soak for 8 to 12 hours.

Pull the bag from the bowl and drain off the soaking water.

Leave the lentils in the bag but untie the top. Fold it back and let water run over your sprouts while moving them around (place your hand at the bottom of the bag and lightly knead).

If you are camping or have limited water, you can refill your soaking container and swirl the hemp bag around to wet all the lentils. I tend to not only swirl but gently massage to make sure each lentil is reached.

Retie the bag and hang to dry. If you are camping, you can swing the bag around to remove most of the water.

Continue rinsing and draining until the sprouts are ready to your liking. The hemp bag does not make a good storage device for finished lentils. You'll want to move to a plastic bag or lidded container.

Be sure to check my recipes for Marinated Lentils and Marinated Quinoa Salad for perfect no-cook travel food.

Recipes

The options are almost endless for using your sprouts. Add your small seed sprouts to salads, sandwiches, smoothies, sushi, omelets, and more. Larger sprouts, such as grains, beans, nuts, and large seeds, are tasty salad additions. Sprouts are great for any place you want a bit of fresh veggie goodness.

Sprouted beans can be used in just about any recipe calling for beans. Hard sprouted beans take 30 minutes to an hour on the stovetop to be soft and creamy. I recommend tasting the sprouted beans every few minutes the first time you cook a new variety.

Once you get the hang of cooking with sprouted beans, try your favorite alternative-cooking methods such as the crockpot, Instant Pot (they are ready in only a few minutes), woodstove, hay box, or Sun Oven (my summertime favorite).

I'm including a few of my favorite recipes to get your started. These are recipes I use in my everyday kitchen. Many are well suited for food storage or emergency cooking with minor adaptations. Most recipes greatly benefit from the addition of fresh produce from the garden or the use of fresh dairy.

Winter Salad

A lovely and simple combination. This can even be used with apples or carrots that are slightly less than stellar. The dressing, and letting the flavors set and meld, helps bring them back to life. I don't usually peel the apples, but if skins are an issue, feel free to remove them.

- 4 carrots, peeled and grated
- 4 apples, cut in bite-size pieces
- Ginger Dressing (recipe below)
- Sprouts (radish, broccoli, alfalfa, or a mix)

Mix together carrots and apples, then toss with Ginger Dressing. Move to the fridge until ready to serve. Add a generous portion of fresh sprouts to each serving when plating.

Ginger Dressing

- ½ cup (homemade) mayonnaise
- ½ cup cultured buttermilk
- ½ tablespoon fresh ginger, grated (or ¼ teaspoon ginger powder)
- 1 clove garlic, finely minced (or ¼ teaspoon garlic powder)

- Sea salt and pepper, to taste
- 1 to 3 tablespoons water (for thinning)

Mix mayonnaise, buttermilk, ginger, and garlic together. Stir in salt and pepper to taste. Add in the water to make a thinner dressing.

Marinated Lentils

This is a great no-cook option. A little like a salad, you can use them as a topper for greens, stuff them in a pita shell or wrap, or eat as is. It's easy to mix it up the night before or the morning of.

The longer it sits, the more time the flavors have to develop. But you can, of course, mix it up and serve immediately. It will still taste great. Feel free to double and enjoy over several meals.

- 3 tablespoons extra-virgin olive oil
- 2 ½ tablespoons red wine vinegar (or to taste)
- 1 tablespoon lemon juice
- 1 ½ teaspoons mustard
- 1 ½ teaspoons pure maple syrup, honey, or granulated natural sugar
- 1 teaspoon sea salt (or to taste)
- ¼ teaspoon black pepper
- 1 to 1 ½ cups green onions (about 1 bunch), thinly sliced, dark and light green parts
- ⅓ cup fresh parsley, minced★
- 1 cup tomatoes, diced (fresh or canned, well drained)
- 3 cups lentils, sprouted at least two days

In a large bowl, whisk together the oil, vinegar, lemon juice, mustard, maple syrup, salt, and pepper. Stir in the green onions, parsley, tomatoes, and lentil sprouts. Season with additional salt and pepper to taste.

★Fresh parsley is best in this recipe, but you can also use dried parsley that is rehydrated and well drained.

Marinated Quinoa Salad

This is a road trip favorite. It's the perfect salad for times when you find yourself without cooking facilities. You do need to plan ahead in order to sprout the quinoa, but not terribly much time since quinoa sprouts rather quickly.

We find this to be a very filling salad. As written, this recipe is more than enough for a hearty lunch or supper. Store leftovers in the fridge or a cooler. Leftovers are even better the next day.

- ½ cup olive oil, plus additional olive oil if desired
- 2 tablespoons tamari (or soy sauce or use a few squirts of coconut aminos)
- 2 teaspoons apple cider vinegar
- Juice of ½ lime or lemon
- 2 cloves garlic, minced
- 2 cups sprouted quinoa
- ¼ teaspoon sea salt
- ¼ cup fresh mint, crushed (or 1 tablespoon dried mint)
- 1 to 3 cups mix-ins (see below)
- Sea salt and pepper, to taste
- Mixed greens (optional)
- Fresh lemon or lime wedges (optional)

In a bowl, combine olive oil, tamari, apple cider vinegar, juice, garlic, and sprouted quinoa. Allow to marinate for 10 to 20 minutes (use this time to prepare mix-in items).

Add all mix-ins. Stir gently. Salt and pepper to taste and add additional olive oil if you would like more of a "dressing." Serve over mixed greens if desired. Squeeze fresh lemon or lime wedges over each salad prior to serving.

Mix-Ins

This salad is a great way to use up small amounts of produce, cheese, and/or meats. Use any combination of the suggestions or anything that sounds good to you. Prepare the mix-ins by cutting into bite-sized pieces if necessary.

Produce

- Sweet pepper (green, red, yellow, etc.)
- Tomatoes (regular or cherry)
- Cucumber
- Celery
- Swiss chard stems (use the greens in a different dish)
- Onion (green, red, white, etc.)
- Broccoli
- Cauliflower
- Carrots
- Jicama
- Radishes
- Avocado

Cheese

- Any flavor of hard cheese, cut in chunks or shredded
- Blue cheese, crumbles or chunks
- Feta
- Goat cheese, crumbles or chunks

Nuts, seeds, and dried fruits

- Any combination of any type

Meats

- Leftover roast, steak, chicken, etc.

- Salmon (fermented, canned, smoked, or leftover)
- Tuna
- Sardines

Grocery (for the times when you can't find fresh items)

- Pimentos
- Marinated artichoke hearts
- Olives (black, green, mixture)
- Water chestnuts
- Hearts of palm
- Roasted red peppers
- Canned beans (your choice of variety)
- Canned fish (tuna, salmon, sardines, etc.)

Sprouted Goodness Nourish Bowl Formula

Nourish Bowls—also called Buddha bowls, bliss bowls, hippie bowls, balanced plates, and several other names—have become popular in recent years. These filling, one-dish meals follow a basic formula for combining whole grains, vegetables, greens, beans, meat (sometimes), toppings, and a dressing.

Sprouts are the perfect addition to nourish bowls since they lend themselves to cooking for a crowd. You can assemble the basic ingredients, and your family or guests can create their own bowls.

The key to making this dish come together quickly is having as many ingredients prepared in advance as possible. Using sprouts means part of the work is already done for you! These bowls are also a great way to use up leftovers.

Here's your basic Nourish Bowl formula:

- Grain: sprouted quinoa, millet, wheat, rice, rye, or barley, or choose their unsprouted counterparts.
- Bean: sprouted lentils, chickpeas, pinto, black, white, or split peas, or choose their unsprouted counterparts.
- Greens: salad greens, cabbage (purple or green), kale★, mustard greens, collard, Swiss chard, etc.
- Vegetable: consider a combination of starchy and non-starchy vegetables and cooked and uncooked. Just about anything works.
- Meat or other protein (optional): beef, chicken, pork, fish, or eggs are all good choices.
- Toppings or treats: crispy nuts or seeds, coconut flakes, fresh herbs, sesame seeds, avocado slices, shredded cheese, Craisins, raisins, and so much more.
- Sauce or dressing: your favorite salad dressing, salsa, tahini sauce, hummus, peanut sauce, pesto, chimichurri sauce, or a simple drizzle of olive oil and a squirt of lemon or lime.

Advanced preparation is the key to these bowls or plates. With the basic formula, you could easily prep the ingredients on a Sunday afternoon and eat bowls all week, enjoying something different each day.

Here are a few preparation tips:

- Grains: if using unsprouted grains, cook per usual instructions. Sprouted quinoa or millet can be used raw or lightly steamed. Sprouted wheat, rice, rye, or barley should be steamed or cooked until soft.
- Beans: unsprouted beans should be soaked and cooked until soft. Sprouted hard beans should be cooked until soft. Sprouted lentils can be lightly steamed or used raw. If using mung beans, they can be treated as lentils and enjoyed raw or steamed. Mung beans are lovely sauteed in a little oil.
- Greens: your greens can be raw, cooked, or a combination. Spring mix or head lettuce are best enjoyed raw. Thinly sliced cabbage is another great raw option, in small amounts. Kale and other heavy leafy greens are popular raw but are best when cooked due to their goitrogenic compounds that increase the need for iodine. If these heavy greens are consumed raw in large amounts, they can affect thyroid function. While I do add these raw to bowls and salads, I don't make these the focus and choose to alternate with lighter, high-water greens. Also, I would not choose to eat a salad or bowl containing uncooked kale, spinach, or other heavy greens every night.
- Vegetable: any raw vegetable you enjoy in a salad works well in these bowls. Tomatoes, cucumber, carrots, celery, bell pepper, green onion, red onion, snow peas, just about anything. Cooked or sauteed vegetables are also nice—spiralized zucchini, sauteed mushrooms, sauteed onions, steamed broccoli or cauliflower, cooked carrots...you name it. Another fabulous idea is roasted veggies, such as beets, sweet potato, onion, cabbage steaks, broccoli, butternut squash. There are so many options. Feel free to combine raw, cooked, and roasted.
- Meat or other protein: before we go any further, yes, the combination of a whole grain and a bean does equal a complete

protein. You can leave off the meat and stick with a plant-based bowl. Or feel free to add shredded roast, cooked ground beef, shredded or diced chicken, a beautiful fillet of salmon or other fish, hard-boiled egg slices, canned salmon or tuna, or even a fried egg over top. Any additional protein works, just cook it before plopping it in your bowl.

- Toppings and treats: these beauties need little advanced preparation. Follow my instructions in this book for making Crispy Nuts or Seeds in the "Nuts and Large Seeds" chapter. Nuts should be chopped to become more of a garnish. You can also snip some fresh herbs, slice an avocado, shred or crumble your favorite cheese.
- Sauce or dressing: mix up your choice of dressing before you start assembling. Or use a store-bought version if that's how you roll. My recipe for Simple Bean Dip can double as a sauce with a few minor tweaks. Check the recipe for more info.

Assembly

Though touted as Nourish Bowls, you can totally use a plate instead. I'll admit I like the bowl concept and tend to choose a larger bowl than I probably should. But it's all healthy, right? Mm-hmm.

1. Place the grain in the bowl or on the plate.
2. Arrange a pile of raw or cooked greens along one side.
3. Arrange a pile of raw or cooked veggies on the other side.
4. Arrange a pile of beans on yet another side.
5. Add your meat to the final side.
6. Sprinkle toppings over it all.
7. Finish with your sauce or dressing.

Or do it my husband's way and just start piling things on. There's no wrong way to assemble your Nourish Bowl.

*To make raw kale easier to chew and to up the flavor, try this massage method. Chop the kale and add a teaspoon or two of olive oil. Squeeze on a little lemon or lime juice (bottled is fine) and sprinkle with salt.

Massage with your hands for a minute or two to distribute. Store for up to five days in a plastic bag.

Please Note: this does not help with the goitrogenic compounds in kale and other leafy greens. To eliminate those, heavy raw greens need to be simmered for 8 minutes. After simmering, I like to toss them with onions that were sautéing in a little healthy fat. Delicious! You can also ferment kale, spinach, cabbage, and other heavy greens to use in your Nourish Bowl.

Sprouted Lentil Patties

These are something like an Egg Foo Yung. For a more authentic dish, top with Asian Sauce.

- 4 cups sprouted lentils
- ½ onion, sliced very thin
- 2 cups leftover sautéed cabbage (or use raw cabbage sliced very thin)
- 2 carrots, shredded
- 6 eggs, beaten
- ½ teaspoon sea salt
- ¼ teaspoon black pepper
- Healthy fat for frying

Steam lentils for up to 10 minutes to soften. Allow to cool slightly.

Combine lentils, onion, cabbage, and carrots. In a separate bowl, beat eggs and then add salt and pepper. Pour eggs over vegetable mixture and stir to incorporate.

Heat a skillet and add your healthy fat. Cook the vegetables like small pancakes. Cook for about 4 or 5 minutes on side one before gently flipping to side two. Cook for an additional couple of minutes. Top with soft cheese, sour cream, or Asian Sauce.

Asian Sauce

- 2 teaspoons cornstarch
- ½ cup beef or chicken broth
- 1 tablespoon soy sauce

Combine all ingredients in a small saucepan. Heat to a boil, stirring constantly. Boil for 1 minute. Serve hot.

Crispy Sprouted Chickpea Tacos

- 2 cups sprouted chickpeas
- ¾ teaspoon sea salt
- ½ to 1 teaspoon chili powder (how spicy do you like it?)
- ½ teaspoon dried oregano
- ½ teaspoon smoked paprika (or regular paprika)
- ½ teaspoon garlic powder
- ½ teaspoon ground cumin
- Pinch of cayenne pepper
- 1 tablespoon healthy fat such as tallow, lard, avocado oil, or coconut oil (may need additional)
- Toppers, such as sour cream, salsa, shredded cheese, lettuce, Crispy Slaw (recipe below), etc.
- Tortillas (sourdough, flour, or corn)

Steam the sprouted chickpeas until soft but not mushy. You want them al dente. This takes anywhere from 3 to 10 minutes, depending on how well sprouted your beans are.

While the chickpeas are steaming, combine the sea salt, chili powder, oregano, paprika, garlic powder, cumin, and cayenne pepper in a small bowl. Set aside.

When they are properly steamed, remove from heat and rinse the beans under cool water. Transfer the steamed, rinsed chickpeas to a clean dish towel. Dry the chickpeas by covering with the towel and gently moving them around to remove as much water as possible.

Turn on your oven to its lowest setting. Use it to warm the tortillas (or warm them in a skillet or over an open flame), plus to keep the chickpeas warm as you cook.

Heat a cast-iron skillet over medium heat and add about ½ tablespoon of healthy fat. Spread the oil by either using a paper towel or tilting the pan so it gives a thin coating over the entire surface.

When the oil is hot, add a portion of the chickpeas. You want a single layer with space between the beans to allow them to sear and crisp. If you overcrowd, they'll steam rather than brown. Cook without stirring for 2 to 3 minutes. Stir the beans.

Add a portion of the spice blend. You will use all of the spice blend, so estimate how much you should use based on how many chickpeas still need to be cooked. Toss the chickpeas in the spices and cook for another few minutes. They should be well coated and nicely browned.

Remove the crispy chickpeas from the skillet, moving to a baking pan and placing in the warm oven. Add additional fat to the skillet as needed and repeat the process until all sprouted chickpeas are cooked.

Assemble the tacos by placing a warm tortilla on a plate, topping with some of the crispy chickpeas, then adding your choice of taco toppers. My favorite toppers are Crispy Slaw, sour cream, and salsa.

Crispy Slaw

This quick and crispy slaw is the perfect taco topper. It also works well on burgers or as a side dish.

- 3 cups cabbage, finely sliced (about ¼ of a head)
- ¼ of a red or sweet white onion, finely diced
- ⅓ cup olive oil (mild) or avocado oil
- ¼ cup lime juice
- 1 teaspoon honey
- ½ teaspoon ground cumin
- 1 clove garlic, finely minced (or ¼ teaspoon garlic powder)
- Sea salt, to taste
- Black pepper, to taste

Add the cabbage and onion to a large bowl.

In a separate bowl, combine the oil, lime juice, honey, cumin, garlic, salt, and pepper. Whisk until well combined and slightly emulsified.

Pour dressing over slaw. Toss to combine.

Quinoa Enchilada Baked Eggs

This is a nourishing, protein-rich comfort meal. It's the perfect dish for late winter to early spring when the backyard chickens are starting to produce again, but the garden is yet to provide, and we're still getting most of our greens from sprouting.

It's also a wonderfully adaptable meal. Be sure to read below for variations. This dish is modified from a recipe on *Alaska From Scratch* to utilize sprouted quinoa and lentils.

Note: I make this using 1½ to 2 cups of sprouted quinoa. I adjust the amount of corn based on the quantity of quinoa. Example: 1½ cup quinoa and 1½ cups corn or 2 cups quinoa and 1 cup corn. Essentially, you want a total of 3 cups between the quinoa and corn.

- 1 ½ to 2 cups sprouted quinoa
- 2 cups sprouted lentils
- 1 to 1 ½ cups corn (either from a can or frozen and slightly thawed)
- ½ teaspoon sea salt, divided, plus additional to taste
- 1 teaspoon ground cumin

- ½ teaspoon garlic powder
- ¼ teaspoon black pepper, plus additional to taste
- 2 teaspoons olive oil or avocado oil
- 1 tablespoon lime juice
- 2 cups enchilada sauce (see recipe below or use store-bought)
- ½ cup cheese, shredded (optional; cheddar, Colby, Monterey, etc.)
- 6 eggs

Preheat oven to 375°.

In a large mixing bowl, combine sprouted quinoa, lentils, and corn. Sprinkle with half of the sea salt and stir.

In a second, smaller dish, combine remaining salt, cumin, garlic powder, black pepper, oil, and lime juice.

Mix the spices with the sprouts and corn.

Add the mixture to a well-seasoned and lightly greased 10" cast-iron skillet*. Top with enchilada sauce, then sprinkle with cheese.

Crack an egg into a small dish. Make a well in the quinoa mixture. then gently add the egg to the well. Repeat until all eggs are used, spacing out the eggs somewhat evenly.

Season eggs with additional salt and pepper.

Bake in preheated oven for 30 minutes, until egg whites are set and quinoa mixture is hot and bubbly. Feel free to bake a few additional minutes if you like your yolks to be hard baked.

Top with your favorite taco or enchilada toppings, such as additional cheese, sour cream, salsa, or minced onion.

*This should work in an 8" or 12" skillet too. You may not have room for 6 eggs in an 8", but if using a 12", you could probably fit in a couple additional eggs.

Variations

I love the convenience of using raw sprouted quinoa and raw sprouted lentils, but this recipe is also delicious using cooked quinoa and cooked beans or sprouted and cooked hard beans (black, pinto, white, etc.).

You could even mix it up and use sprouted quinoa with cooked beans or cooked quinoa with sprouted beans. Have leftover cooked rice or barley? Use it in place of the quinoa. No eggs? Leave them out.

The combination of the grain and beans will still give you plenty of protein and nourishment, especially if you use my homemade enchilada sauce below. The sky truly is the limit with this adaptable dish.

All the Rave Enchilada Sauce

Oh, mercy. This is the perfect enchilada sauce. Perfectly spiced and made with nourishing bone broth, it's not too hot and is full of flavor. I found this enchilada sauce recipe years ago on Rockin' Robin's website. I've adapted it slightly.

- ¼ cup whole wheat flour or sprouted flour
- 3 tablespoons butter, coconut oil, or tallow (or use half butter and half olive oil)
- 2 cups bone broth (chicken or beef is best, but pork works too)
- 1 tablespoon chili powder (use less or more, depending on how hot you like it)
- 1 teaspoon ground cumin
- 2 teaspoons garlic powder
- 1 teaspoon sea salt*
- 1 pinch ground cinnamon

- ¼ teaspoon Sucanat or another dry sweetener

Melt the butter or oil in a medium saucepan over low heat. When hot, slowly whisk in the flour, stirring constantly. You want the flour to cook a little to increase the flavor. Add the chili powder and whisk well.

Add the broth a little at a time, whisking well after each addition. As it starts to thin out, allow it to cook a minute or two before adding more. I've found that slowly adding the full two cups results in a richer sauce.

Once all the broth is added, add the remaining ingredients. Increase the heat and bring to a boil, stirring occasionally.

Allow to boil for 3 to 5 minutes. The sauce will begin to thicken during this time.

Remove from heat. Use immediately or refrigerate for later use. When allowed to set, a skin forms on top of the sauce. You can stir this in or peel it off and throw away.

Use this sauce in any recipe that calls for enchilada sauce.

*I use homemade, unsalted broth. If you use a broth with salt added, you will want to use less salt. I'd recommend starting with none and tasting as the sauce cooks.

Impossible Tamale Pie

This delicious dish combines two of my traditional food favorites: sprouts and sourdough. You may remember Impossible Sweet Pies, where the crust is poured over the fruit, separating it into layers. It's so easy since there's no rolling of the dough. This uses the exact same concept for a fabulous, savory dish.

I use sprouted lentils, which, when cooked, take on a consistency and flavor somewhat reminiscent of ground beef. Okay, okay...I'm not fooling anyone into thinking this is a meat-based pie, but it truly is delicious. Even my meat-loving husband and son agree.

This recipe works great in a 10" well-seasoned cast-iron skillet. A 12" skillet should also work without adjustments. If you use an 8", evaluate the amount of filling before mixing up the crust. You may need to scoop out a little (serve it on the side) before adding the crust so it doesn't run over and result in more crust than filling.

Pie Filling

- ½ medium onion, diced
- 1 tablespoon healthy fat, divided (butter, lard, tallow, coconut oil)
- 1 tablespoon chili powder (how spicy do you like it? Feel free to add more or less)
- 1 teaspoon cumin
- 1 teaspoon paprika (regular or smoky)
- ¾ teaspoon sea salt
- ¼ teaspoon black pepper
- ¼ teaspoon oregano
- 3 cups sprouted lentils
- ½ cup corn (frozen or canned)
- 1 (4-ounce) can diced green chilis (optional)
- ½ cup cheddar cheese, shredded (optional)

Impossible Crust

- 1½ cups sourdough starter, fed within the last 12 hours
- 3 eggs
- 1 teaspoon sea salt
- 1 teaspoon basil
- ½ teaspoon baking soda

Preheat oven to 375°.

Sauté onion in ½ tablespoon fat until soft.

In a small bowl, combine the spices. Set aside.

When the onion is soft, add the rest of the fat, lentils, and corn. Stir to coat and melt the fat. Sprinkle the spice blend over the top and stir to mix well. Let cook for a few minutes, stirring occasionally to blend the spices over everything. Add the can of chilis. Stir to combine. Sprinkle with cheese. Turn off heat while you mix up the crust.

In a medium-sized bowl, combine the sourdough starter and eggs. Whisk well until the eggs are incorporated. Stir in the salt. Sprinkle the baking soda over the top and stir to combine. Gently pour over the lentil mixture.

Bake for 20 to 25 minutes until the crust is lightly browned and a toothpick comes back clean.

To serve, cut into wedges and top with your favorite taco toppings: sour cream, salsa, shredded lettuce, shredded cheese, olives, green onion, etc.

Egg Tortilla Wrap

When I was in fifth grade, my class had a sandwich-making contest. We were supposed to make our favorite sandwich at home and bring it in. The best sandwich would win a prize.

Sadly, I neglected to mention the contest until the night before. It must have been shopping time because we didn't have any bread. My mom suggested a family favorite: hard-fried egg wrapped in a tortilla and topped with alfalfa sprouts. Yes, I do find it amusing we had no bread in the house but had sprouts. I can't explain it.

My sandwich won second place. I'm sure it would have won first if the egg would have been warm. Over the years, I've tinkered with the sandwich. This version is my all-time favorite for a quick breakfast or lunch.

- 1 egg
- 1 tablespoon milk
- 1 pinch salt
- 1 dash black pepper
- 1 dash hot sauce (optional)
- 1 teaspoon butter, ghee, tallow, unflavored coconut oil or your favorite fat
- 2+ tablespoons cheese, shredded (any type)
- 1 small (6-inch) tortilla
- A smear of mayonnaise and/or mustard (optional)
- ¼ to ½ cup radish, alfalfa, broccoli, or your favorite "green" sprout

In a small bowl, whisk together the egg, milk, salt, pepper, and hot sauce. Preheat a small skillet (I use a well-seasoned, 6" cast-iron). Add the tortilla to the skillet during the preheat stage so it will warm slightly and become pliable. Once the skillet and tortilla are warm, move the tortilla to a plate.

56

Add the fat and allow to melt, tilting to coat. Add the egg mixture and tilt so the egg covers the bottom of the pan. Let cook for about 30 seconds to 1 minute, then carefully flip to cook the other side. Don't worry if you scramble it in the process. Top with shredded cheese.

Add a smear of mayo and/or mustard to your tortilla. Top with the egg and cheese mixture. Layer on green sprouts. Roll up and enjoy.

Tuna Rolls

My son loves all things Japanese, including sushi, so we make a variety of sushi-like rolls at home. This simple Tuna Roll makes a delicious lunch and is one of our favorites. It's also a great use of leftover rice.

The bamboo mat makes rolling the sushi easier, but it can be rolled using parchment paper or plastic wrap. It's not as easy and doesn't hold as tightly, but it still works. If you're new to rolling, there are a lot of videos available on the internet to show you how to do it. *Pro tip:* Cut all of the vegetables before reheating the rice.

- 1 cup rice, previously cooked (white, brown, jasmine, basmati, etc.)
- ½ cup water, divided
- 1½ tablespoon rice wine vinegar
- A sprinkle of sugar (optional; I use a less processed sugar, like Sucanat)
- 1 can Albacore tuna, drained
- 1 to 2 tablespoons mayonnaise
- A sprinkle of garlic powder
- ½ ripe avocado, thinly sliced
- 1 carrot, grated
- ½ cucumber, seeded and cut into strips (optional)
- ¼ bell pepper, cut lengthwise in thin strips (optional; red is beautiful but green tastes just as good)
- 3 cups alfalfa, radish, clover, or other "green" sprout
- 3 nori sheets

Make the pseudo sushi rice: Reheat cooked rice with ¼ cup of the water. Cover with a lid but keep an eye on it so it doesn't stick. After a few minutes, give it a stir. Add the remaining ¼ cup of water, rice wine vinegar, and a sprinkle of sugar. Stir and heat through. Your rice should be somewhat sticky. Set aside and let cool slightly.

In a small bowl, combine tuna, mayo, and garlic powder. Mix well. I like the tuna to be fairly broken up and somewhat smooth.

Lay one sheet of nori on a bamboo mat, shiny side down.

Put ⅓ of the rice on the nori sheet, spreading gently with the back of a spoon. You want to cover to the edges and flatten the rice, but don't smash it. The rice will "seal" the roll.

Add ⅓ of the prepared tuna, about an inch or so from the edge nearest you. Add a few pieces of avocado, some grated carrot, some of the cucumber, and bell pepper (divide the vegetables in thirds so each roll will receive a portion). Top with 1 cup of sprouts (I don't measure, just eyeball it).

Beginning on the edge closest to you, roll tightly, making sure to "tuck" the fillings as you go. Move the roll to a cutting board.

Roll the remaining two.

Use a sharp knife to cut the rolls. I cut in half and then cut each half in thirds.

Variation: Spicy Tuna Roll

Add a squirt of Sriracha sauce to the mayonnaise when mixing the tuna. Proceed with the recipe as written.

I like making a Sriracha/mayo sauce for dipping too. Combine ¼ cup of mayo with a few squirts of Sriracha (how hot do you like it?!), then add a drop or two of soy sauce and mix well. You can dip your cut pieces of sushi in the sauce or spread more sauce on top of each piece.

2-Ingredient Sprouted Bread

So easy! Just two ingredients give you a delicious, sweet-tasting loaf. This is fabulous cooked in the crockpot, resulting in a super moist bread. You can also cook it in the oven or on top of a woodstove.

- 1 cup sprouted wheat
- ½ teaspoon sea salt

Put the two ingredients in a food processor. Pulse until it's chopped enough to stick together so you can form your loaf, then pulse a little more. I like it to be a somewhat smooth dough, with few wheat kernels left, but you may prefer something a little chunkier.

Note: If it's not pulsed enough, it will crumble after baking. You may wish to pulse it very smooth the first time and adjust on future batches.

If using a crockpot, shape to fit, then cook on low for 8 hours.

If using an oven, lightly grease a cookie sheet. Shape into a round, baguette, rolls, breadsticks, etc. Bake in a low-heat oven, around 225°, until cooked through, maybe somewhere around an hour. This will vary depending on your loaf. Small loaves (buns) will cook quicker.

To cook on the top of the woodstove, use a Dutch oven or spider (the kind of Dutch oven with the little legs) with a lid. Put your loaf in another container that will fit inside the oven. I use a round 8" cake pan.

Heat the Dutch oven with the lid in place on the woodstove while you are processing your wheat. Carefully move the cake pan (or similar container) to the warm Dutch oven and replace the lid. Bake until cooked through. How long? This will depend on how hot your fire is and how large your loaf is.

You can scale this recipe up, but you may need to process it in batches depending on your food processor.

Sprouted, Fermented, and Dehydrated Dosa Crackers

Tasty and delicious! This is a great way to use leftover sprouted grains, beans, or a combination. This recipe is adapted from Traditional Cooking School Fundamentals eCourse. Learn more at HomespunOasis.com/TCS.

- 2 cups sprouted grains and/or beans
- ½ cup water, plus additional as needed
- 1 tablespoon apple cider vinegar
- 1 teaspoon sea salt, plus additional to taste
- Optional seasonings as desired, such as black pepper, cumin, garlic powder, onion powder, paprika, chili powder, curry powder, cayenne pepper, etc.

In a food processor or blender, pulse sprouted grains and/or beans with water, apple cider vinegar, salt, and optional seasonings until smooth. If needed, add more water, 1 tablespoon at a time, until mixture is a thick, pancake-batter consistency.

Taste and adjust seasonings. Put mixture in a jar or glass bowl, leaving at least 1" of space below the top of the container. Cover with a lid and let ferment at room temperature for one day.

Line dehydrator tray(s) with parchment paper or liners. Spread batter in a thin, even layer about ¼" thick, in small circles or in a continuous layer. If desired, sprinkle with additional sea salt (a heavier grind is nice) or seasonings.

Dehydrate until dry and crispy, turning every few hours. When you reach your desired crispness, remove and let cool completely. Store in an airtight container.

Simple Bean Dip

A delicious and simple bean dip or spread that's perfect with veggies, Dosa crackers, sourdough crackers, or flatbread wedges.

- 1 cup sprouted pinto, chickpea, white, or black beans (or a combination if that's how you roll)
- ¼ cup water
- ¼ teaspoon sea salt
- Scant ¼ teaspoon garlic powder
- Dash or two black pepper
- ¼ teaspoon ground cumin
- 1 tablespoon Parmesan cheese (the kind from a can is fine)
- 1 teaspoon lemon juice
- 1 tablespoon extra-virgin olive oil

Mix all ingredients in a food processor. Check for consistency. You may need to add a little water, 1 tablespoon at a time. You can keep processing until fully smooth or leave it a little chunky; the choice is yours!

This can be served cold (best with chickpeas, think hummus) or warm (fabulous when using pinto or black beans). If serving warm, you can add shredded cheddar cheese and a dash or two of your favorite hot sauce. Either way is yummy.

Variation

Simple Bean Dip also works as a simple sauce with just a few tweaks. To 1 cup cold bean dip (any variety), add 2 teaspoons Dijon mustard, 2 teaspoons Sucanat (or Rapadura or maple syrup). Whisk together until smooth.

Now evaluate your sauce. It probably needs to be thinner. Add water, 1 tablespoon at a time, until you reach your desired consistency. Try this sauce on your Sprouted Goodness Nourish Bowl.

Resources

Check out the Resources page that goes along with this book for more recipes, information, and helpful tools: HomespunOasis.com/Sprouts

Find more sprouting information and recipes on my website: HomespunOasis.com

Also by Millie Copper

Get 20% off Millie Copper's nonfiction eBooks at HomespunOasis.com/Books with coupon code SAVE20.

Sourdough for Your Food Storage: Add Nutrition and Variety to Your Baked Goods

Want to make tasty treats your whole family will love? Are you looking for a great way to expand your food storage grains?

Sourdough For Your Food Storage will show you how! Not only will you learn how to make delicious, crusty breads, but also biscuits, main dishes, and even desserts! Sourdough is a healthier alternative to yeast, and it tastes great to boot.

Real Food Hits the Road: Budget-Friendly Tips, Ideas, and Recipes for Enjoying Real Food Away from Home

Are you planning to hit the road for a family vacation? Do you want to take a road trip, but the idea of eating out three meals a day doesn't work for your budget or your health?

Real Food Hits the Road will be your guide to saving the budget, keeping your digestion working well, and eating real food away from home while letting you enjoy the trip and not "cook" all of the time.

Stock the Real Food Pantry: Save Money and Time While Gaining Peace of Mind

Do you want to stock your pantry with nutritious food your family will actually eat? In these trying times, are you focusing on your food storage?

If so, *Stock the Real Food Pantry* has you covered. Learn how a wonderfully stocked real food pantry will save you money and time—while giving you peace of mind.

Design a Dish: Save Your Food Dollars!

Would you like to learn great methods to reduce food waste? What if you could enjoy one meal for "free" each week?

Design a Dish will teach you how to make wonderful, simple dishes you can prepare day in and day out. You'll be amazed at how easy it is to nourish your family with these tasty dishes!

Stretchy Beans: Nutritious, Economical Meals the Easy Ways

Do you struggle with feeding your family delicious, healthy meals? Are you tired of trying to figure out what's for dinner each night? Do you cringe when you see how much money your family spends on groceries each month?

If so, *Stretchy Beans* is the solution you've been looking for! Learn how to easily prepare dinners that the whole family will love—while staying on budget, spending less time in the kitchen, and not losing your sanity.

About the Author

Millie Copper, writer of Cozy Apocalyptic Fiction and preparedness mentor, was born in Nebraska but never lived there. Her parents fully embraced wanderlust and moved regularly, giving her an advantage of being from nowhere and everywhere.

As an adult, Millie is fully rooted in a solar-powered home in the wilds of Wyoming with her husband and young son, milking ornery goats and tending chickens on their small homestead. In their free time, they escape to the mountains for a hike or laze along the bank of the river to catch their dinner. Four adult daughters, three sons-in-law, and three grandchildren round out the family.

Since 2009, Millie has authored articles on traditional foods, alternative health, homesteading, and preparedness—many times all within the same piece. Millie has penned five nonfiction, traditional food focused books, sharing how, with a little creativity, anyone can transition to a real foods diet without overwhelming their food budget.

The twelve-installment *Havoc in Wyoming* Christian Post-Apocalyptic fiction series uses her homesteading, off-the-grid, and preparedness lifestyle as a guide. The adventure continues with the *Montana Mayhem* series.

Find Millie at www.MillieCopper.com
Facebook: www.facebook.com/MillieCopperAuthor/
Amazon: www.amazon.com/author/MillieCopper
BookBub: https://www.bookbub.com/authors/Millie-Copper

www.ingramcontent.com/pod-product-compliance
Lightning Source LLC
Chambersburg PA
CBHW071217120626
46546CB00006B/2604